# PHILIPPE
# Starck

To Misha, Lacey and The Puck.

THIS IS A CARLTON BOOK

Text and design copyright © 1999 Carlton Books Limited

This edition published by Carlton Books Limited 1999
20 St Anne's Court
Wardour Street
London
W1V 3AW

A CIP catalogue for this book is available from the British Library

ISBN 1 85868 738 1

EXECUTIVE EDITOR: Sarah Larter
MANAGING ART EDITOR: Zoë Mercer
DESIGN: Simon Mercer
PICTURE RESEARCH: Alex Pepper
PRODUCTION: Garry Lewis

Printed and bound in Dubai

# PHILIPPE
# Starck

JUDITH CARMEL-ARTHUR

**CARLTON**

For twenty years Philippe Starck's career has been the subject of a virtual cacophony of accolades. Now counted among the best-known and most widely publicized of contemporary international designers, Starck, who was born in Paris, January 18, 1949, was recognized initially for his stylish interiors. A commission in the early 1980s for a redesign of President Mitterrand's private quarters in the Elysée Palace, Paris, catapulted his work into international critical focus. Starck quickly claimed a position as one of the late-twentieth century's most prolific and challenging architect-designers and his celebrity status arose as an almost immediate result.

Starck then went on to produce a series of provocative, often luxuriously avant-garde interiors including the Starck Club in Dallas (1982), the Café Costes, Paris (1984; closed 1994), the Manin Restaurant, Tokyo (1987), and the now famous Royalton Hotel, New York (1988). The Café Costes, dominated by its axial, theatrical staircase, and the Royalton, an essay in sheer elegance, invited international attention for their compellingly stylish, postmodern interpretations of interior, public space. Both quickly became pilgrimage sites frequented by devotees of the 1980s designer cult, and set trends within the interior design establishment. Much has been said in the press about Starck's membership in the late twentieth century "cult of celebrity"; and on his ability to capitalize upon this popular, public predilection for urbane elegance. With compliance, he has created environments in which people want to be seen and are seen, proving the ultimate success of his particular version of cosmopolitan spectacle.

But the critical press itself has consistently both aided and abetted Starck's climb to celebrity status. They have, paradoxically, heroised his name itself by recasting it in nimble

# PHILIPPE

linguistic variations in order to attract competitive readership. Titles such as "The Art of Starckiness", "Philippe Le Roi", "Starck Contrasts", "Starck Truths", "Starck Lite, Starck Brite", "Starck Staring" and "Starck Treatment" have merely served to exacerbate celebrity, while paralleling Starck's own application of his name to his designs in the 1990s. Perhaps the most effective examples are the two recent garments for Wolford: "Starck Naked" (1998) and "Starck Naked Hot" (1999). But numerous other examples arise in the product range covered by the new *Good Goods* catalogue (1998), including transport and recreational products such as "Kayak Starck" (with Rotomod) and "Cruiser Starck" (with Blauwerk). By means of product names such as these, Starck linguistically consolidates his identity, ensuring his works can not be verbally recalled without reference to the designer himself. By labelling, he establishes pedigree.

"IN A WAY, **I think** THAT IT HAS BECOME THE JOB OF **DESIGNERS** TO SPEND MORE AND MORE OF THEIR TIME PRODUCING **signs** ... AND LESS AND LESS OF IT ON PRODUCING ACTUAL **OBJECTS**."

PHILIPPE STARCK, *INTERNATIONAL DESIGN YEARBOOK*, 1978–9

There are a number of notions which can be extracted from Starck's "messaging". Labelling is used as a means of focusing upon design origin and provenance. In doing so, Starck celebrates a conceptual triumph of fashion over function, an expression of our

# S T A R C K

current cultural climate. It perhaps equally recalls something of Starck's early years (1971–72) as the Art Director of the Pierre Cardin fashion house in Paris. In the international mass marketing of "designer" goods, the label, often carrying the designer's signature, is worth its weight in gold. Rather than "signing" the outcome of his design endeavours, Starck takes this form of labelling one step further, literally naming the product in his own image. As a marketing strategy, he thus exploits the cult of object labelling to deplete goods of their primary functional significance, translating them into artefacts of private worship and public envy, while simultaneously infusing them with more fantasy than fact. Much as he may chose to deny it, the *Good Goods* catalogue is replete with such aspirational icons of conspicuously "labelled" consumption.

Throughout his career, naming has been a consistent postmodernist device used by Starck to invest his products with anthropomorphic qualities, taming them, giving them a somewhat perverse familiarity on the consumer's behalf. Nearly all of his furniture bears quirky names such as Mister Bliss (1982 for XO) and Boom Rang (1992 for Driade), while his product designs have not been spared: Miss Sissi table and wall lamp (1990 for Flos), Jim Nature portable television set (1994 for Saba) and the Moa Moa bakelite radio (1994 for Saba). Some names appear to delightfully honour his two children: Ara (the Ara III House boat, and the Ara table lamp of 1988 for Flos) and Oa (the Oa table lamp, 1996 for Flos). Other names are said to derive from the science fiction novels by the author Philip K. Dick: "Lola Mundo", "Dole Melipone", "Tippy Jackson". One way or another, this characteristic combines with the prolific nature of Starck's output to suggest we are meant to recognize in his design "virility" identifiable, named progeny – a Starck "family" – which populates both his world and ours.

It has not been enough that his, on the whole, provocative designs speak for themselves. He has spoken on their and his own behalf, and often. He is perhaps the most interviewed of international design celebrities, having positioned himself as the foremost interpreter of his own work. Of the few books and well over 250 articles written about him in recent years, a good number purport as their "text" somewhat extensive Starck interviews. The designer himself has displaced the journalist, as well as the critic in an attempt by publishers, and Starck himself, to describe high-status, contemporary products and interiors in the "designer's own words", thereby getting closer to "authentic" creative motivation.

Starck's interviews are prescriptive. They are timed and formulated for widespread consumption, and talk of what "good" design should be and what it isn't. Their personal illuminations about individual products and projects reveal something of his design approach, and are thus invaluable sources of information:

"ONCE IN A RESTAURANT, THIS vision OF A SQUID-LIKE LEMON SQUEEZER CAME UPON ME, SO I STARTED SKETCHING IT … AND FOUR YEARS LATER IT BECAME QUITE famous. BUT FOR ME IT IS MORE A SYMBOLIC MICRO-SCULPTURE THAN A FUNCTIONAL OBJECT. ITS REAL PURPOSE IS NOT TO SQUEEZE THOUSANDS OF LEMONS BUT TO ENABLE A NEWLYWED TO ENGAGE IN CONVERSATION WITH HIS MOTHER-IN-LAW …"

INTERVIEW WITH MARCELLE KATZ, *SUNDAY TIMES MAGAZINE*

They equally demonstrate some of the more intimate aspects of the life behind design:

"AFTER LUNCH I HAVE A SIESTA. THEN IT'S BACK TO THE DRAWING BOARD WITH MY INFRARED HEADPHONES. I CAN'T WORK WITHOUT music."

Nevertheless, they should also be seen as self-promotional confessionals aimed directly at the pockets of the Starck consumer. In their frequency and availability in the popular design and home decorating press, such interviews can be argued to not only supplement, but rival the actual purchase of tangible goods in importance. They are moderately priced, saleable commodities meant to complement any toothbrush or plastic chair.

It is fair to say that Starck has tried to generate a genuine discourse between himself and the design world. The personal narrative which his numerous interviews provide emphasizes this, and redresses the absence of equally valuable information within the context of contemporary design where we don't hear nearly enough from designers themselves.

The stylistic background of Starck's design vocabulary is staunchly French, with an informed sprinkling of the Art Deco and the American "streamline" aesthetic of the earlier twentieth century. It must be noted that many of his interior ensembles of the late 1980s, particularly those executed in the United States, can and perhaps should be contextualized within an analysis of images of power in American culture at that time. Nancy Reagan's "politics of symbolism" as outlined by Debora Silverman provided the specific cultural framework for, above all, the interior of Manhattan's Royalton Hotel (1988) and its elegantly manipulative furnishings, including: the high-backed couch, long chair, armchair (all 1991; Driade), the wooden chair of 1988 (Driade) and the Royalton bed (1992; Driade). From the outset the hotel's design agenda was loaded with pre-emptive meaning and quickly became a "cultural space" frequented by the high-status design consumer and cognoscenti. In this sense it came to function as a proto-sales environment in which the consumer could experience the pleasure and opulence of Starck's furniture and lighting designs first-hand. The interiors thus gave the products themselves a cultural status beyond that of the hotel lobby, and one in which any subsequent buyer could share at the moment of purchase.

Starck's interiors at the Royalton very neatly fit into what was then becoming a national, but intrinsically anti-historical "aristocratic" design agenda in America under the Reagan administration, and which had conjoined with a powerful advocacy in the guise of Diana Vreeland's bizarre exhibitions of French decorative design at New York's Metropolitan Museum of Art. Starck was by then France's *enfant terrible* of contemporary design, and would have aroused interest in American high society by participating in the remodelling of President Mitterand's private apartments earlier in the decade. His interpretations of interior public space at the Royalton as exclusive, feminine, intimate and organic would have evoked a culture of French luxury and pre-Revolutionary social distinction. This would naturally have appealed to the culture of image with its preferences for fantasy illusion which permeated America's "aristocratic" movement of the late 1980s, especially in New York City.

For the domestic landscape Starck has produced design self-conscious, commercially high-profile artefacts from multiple media. Objects designed, for example, in the early 1990s for Alessi, are meant for a strictly urban clientele, and are directed towards a comparatively cosmopolitan aficionado whose interest is in enjoying the "spectacle" such objects have to offer. Typical of products arising from this postmodernist domestic agenda, the Max de Chinois colander (1990–91; stainless steel and brass), the Ti Tang teapot (white porcelain with aluminium coating), the Su Mi Tang cream jug (white porcelain) and the Mister Meumeu cheese grater (stainless steel and polyamide), all dating from 1992, have been infused during the very process of design with a visual language of cultural references. These often witty, certainly multi-layered signifiers may be more valuable to the consumer than ideas of traditional utility.

Above all, the immensely "masculine" Hot Bertaa kettle (1990–91; plastic and aluminium), an icon of Starck's career and also, by the way, for Alessi, shares significant features with Starck's architecture of the period; including an informed combination of materials, an aggressive architectonic and sculptural quality, the asymmetrical distribution of parts and it's stone-like surface treatment, for example: the maquette for the French

Pavillion, the Maison de France, 1990, at the Venice Biennale; and the drawings for Star's Door, 1992, Parc de Bercy, Paris. Upon purchase, the consumer is not only buying an Alessi product, but more importantly taking home a little bit of Starck himself; a small portion of his architectural vision of the world.

Objects such as this not only make insistent statements about the continuation of the early twentieth-century "machine" aesthetic in both form and surface treatment, but unite – on behalf of the domestic kitchen – the symbolism of structural technology and metals, on the one hand, with that of expressionist architecture on the other. There is something psychologically bleak here; almost futuristic, but darkly so. The strong sculptural presence of the streamlined "teardrop" shape, a leitmotif of Starck's oeuvre – arguably derived from the influence of American designers – which marks the Hot Bertaa and much of his architecture of the period, also has a metamorphic quality. The forms seem to be "emerging" from the ground or from the kitchen counter, while the kettle itself is a version upside-down of the subsequent Bordeaux-Mérignac airport project of 1993, a Control Tower which was a competition design with Luc Arsène Henry Jr.

Above all, the utility value of the clever Hot Bertaa kettle is truly questionable. It is only ostensibly functional, while clearly exemplifying postmodernist "micro-architecture" for the domestic scene. It was intended to become a "design classic" and, like kitchen wares produced by Rosenthal of Germany in the 1960s and 1970s, took on immediate design authority by being targeted not towards the consumer, but towards the design museum. Such objects are highly competitive within the kitchenware/ceramics industry for their kudos value , despite the fact that they remain comparatively poor sellers and often don't work.

Here there appears a distinction within Starck's work: objects that could be loosely categorized as the "masculine" or the "feminine".

The "feminine" strain is inflected less towards Starck's "masculine", boldly sculptural architectural achievements, than towards his furniture dating from the late 1980s onwards.

Much of this shares with his domestic artefacts of approximately the same period a strong biomorphic language of distinctly "feminine"allusions. Sensuous curvilinear forms, evocative organic shapes, and an ethos of intimacy and interiority – of the "salon" – characterize these artefacts in a stereotypically "feminine" manner. Their visual language recalls the naturalistic vocabulary of the eighteenth-century decorative arts in France, and it is no mistake that they also referentially imply the *fin de siècle* Art Nouveau. Starck's national patrimony has provided him with a fertile source of inspiration and quotation, especially within the context of decorative arts history.

Postmodern biomorphism has been regarded as a reaction against the "masculinity" of technology in the waning Machine Age design aesthetic, especially as embodied in the so-called "Hi-Tech" style of the 1980s, of which Starck's harshly rectilinear Sarapis Stool (1986; tubular steel and steel mesh; Driade) has been considered an example. Biomorphism has been argued to represent a cultural regeneration of a more sensorial "femininity" within the interior landscape. As such it represents an attempt to interject into domestic interiors visually softer, more consumer-friendly products which share the familiar plant, animal and even human forms of their owners and environments. The often witty and playful musings of such domestic objects serve to psychologically invite a wider clientele to purchase, while showing that designers such as Starck are attempting to reintroduce human values into domestic product design.

The President M Table of 1981–84 (glass and varnished steel), designed for the bedroom of President Mitterrand's wife in the Elysée Palace, Paris, was among the earliest expressions of biomorphism in Starck's furniture design and may be considered a prefigurement of his later works. The table, which also shows a predilection for simplified and witty structural relationships, was later commercially produced by Baleri for public consumption. The die-cast, "fin"-like appendages supporting the glass top are notable for their subtle biomorphic configurations, parodying the aerofoils that stabilize rockets, while referencing design history in their play on the American styling used by Raymond Loewy and others of the American "streamline" aesthetic. Their comparatively small scale, but essential presence in the otherwise "high tech" design is a crucial indicator of Starck's emerging organic tendencies, which ultimately led to the highly sculptural, albeit "feminized" example of the W.W. Stool of 1990 (aluminium), produced by Vitra, designed for Wim Wenders, the German film director.

The W.W. Stool stands out for its expressive insistence upon the organic. Moreover, like numerous artefacts ultimately bowing to *fin de siècle* France, it acts as a cultural signifier of deeper psychological threads. It talks of impulses of desire – perhaps of purchase – made visible. It hovers uncomfortably between images of dream and those of material reality. The growth metaphor embodied in the forms of the legs and tail of the seat suggests an ongoing debate between reason (function) and emergent emotion (expression). The conscious process of the viewer/user is inhibited from deciding between the two. Interior artefacts such as this undermine any reasoned clarity towards the identity of utilitarian objects, while interjecting a subversive beckoning to the consumer: the hope of transferring from dream into reality the stool's latent embodiment of a domestic "pleasure principle" and all that might imply. In short, the artefact is meant to stimulate the imagination and provoke feelings of desire. It speaks of a late twentieth-century culture of wish-fulfilment.

A series of pieces dating from between those two artefacts shows especially provocative biomorphic and anthropomorphic qualities. These include the Lola Mundo table-cum-chair (1988, cast aluminium and ashwood/ebony finish plywood; Driade); the Louis XX chair (1992, polypropylene and aluminium; Vitra), the Peninsula chair (1995, beechwood with upholstery; XO); Cam El Eon (anodized aluminium and polypropylene/maderon; Driade); and the elegant, stacking chair Olly Tango (1996; chrome tubular steel and bent veneered plywood; Driade).

Varying leitmotifs, some of which seem to behave as dual gender signifiers, fit somewhat uneasily within this category of biomorphic products. The flame, or "streamlined teardrop" motif, said to resemble the wings of a bird or of an aeroplane, has been attributed to paternal influence – Starck's father was an aerodynamics engineer. The theme is as persistent as any within Starck's oeuvre, while its application to as many commercial purposes as possible proves its ability to "mutate" within Starck's own imagination, multiplying its market potential. The sensuality of the form, its inherent litheness and smooth, erotic curvatures firstly imply the "feminine". This is most apparent in the design of artefacts such as the Laguiole Set of stainless steel knives, original designed 1986 (manufactured, 1996; Alessi); Objets Pointus tableware of 1986 (1996; Alessi); toothbrush and holder, 1989 (manufactured by Fluocaril); O'Kelvin table candlestick in polished turned aluminium and glass, original design 1989 (1996; Alessi); Alo, voice-command telephone 1996 (concept by Starck; design by Jérôme Olivet; Thomson); Vase with Flowers, 1990 (1996; marble and glass; Alessi) and Hook telephone, 1996 (ABS plastic; Thomson/Alessi).

However, it is typical of Starck to invest his work with multiple references, and a variation on the "flame" theme metamorphoses into an organic, "spermatoid squiggle" whose most notorious manifestation is the rooftop flame of the Asahi Beer Hall in Tokyo of 1990. Its siblings include the Walter Wayle wall clock (1989; thermoplastic resin; Alessi); Sesamo and Apriti door handles (both 1991; aluminium; Ros Kleis); Olympic Flame lighter (1992; stainless steel); Dr Kiss toothbrush (1998; polyamide, Alessi) in which the teasing twist of the tip behaves as a pert welcome.

Starck's ubiquitous "horn shape" is another motif characterized by an inherent cross-gendering. It's simple and elegant formulation in the Ara chrome plated table lamp of 1988 for Flos belies a vision of interiors populated by objects of gentle, feminine curvatures and aggressive, masculine gestures. It is simultaneously one and the same, the dual embodied in the one; unlike the Lucifer wall sconce (1989; Flos), which is unabashedly phallic in its symbolic implications.

Starck's consistent postmodernist "borrowings" from diverse sources is a self-conscious mark of his showmanship. The blunted, conical base of the Toothbrush for L'Oréal of 1990 acts as a signifier guiding the user/viewer into the realm of sculptural history. The base, or "pedestal", supports what has been rightly argued to be a "Brancusi-like" stem of the toothbrush itself, investing in the design/art-conscious owner a feeling of confident erudition – a reward for recognizing the referential bearings of the object and its quotation from Constantin Brancusi's bronze Bird in Space of 1925.

All of these "gendered" pieces bear relationships with the strongly biomorphic statements of Starck's career, often seen in the now famous three-legged chairs of the 1980s and 1990s. An early version (Costes Chair, 1982; tubular steel and bent ply shell and leather; Driade) was debuted at the Café Costes, Paris in 1984, while the motif achieved international acclaim somewhat later in the W.W. Stool. It also appeared in the early designs in the Dr Sondebar chair (1981; tubular steel; XO), the Miss Dorn chair (1985; black fabric, Disform), Ed Archer ( cast aluminium and sprung steel; Driade) Prattfall (1985, tubular steel with leather, Driade), and in the Tippy Jackson table (1985; tubular steel and turned steel; Driade). Structurally, the three-legged motif betrays Starck's experimentation with furniture "mechanics" and his highly regarded, but underplayed genius as a problem solving technician. In his own right he is a master of rational engineering who is not afraid to negotiate daringly simple solutions; a case in point being the Dole Melipone folding table of 1981 (tubular steel, glass and epoxy; XO).

Starck propagates notions of design as a collective act, and rightly so, but one in which he maintains a creative hierarchy with himself at the top. Previous books on Starck have helped to promote this ideology by including photographic images and portraits of not only Starck and his children, but equally of his friends, collaborators, close associates and patrons, evoking the romance of an extended family. In fact, Starck himself verbally recasts these individuals as his "tribe" in an anthropological posturing. He thus necessarily differentiates between himself together with those who directly support the realization of his personal design agenda, and those who don't. This is tangibly confirmed in the imagery of the chair backs at the Restaurant Felix, Peninsula Hotel (1994, Hong Kong). Each of the Peninsula chairs (1995; XO) boasts the printed, photographic portrait of one of the tribe members, including Starck's daughter Ara, his fiancée Patricia Bailer, and a portrait of Starck himself. This form of homage to his nearest and dearest is also a gesture of objecti-fication. The tribe becomes something which is at once personalized and marketable. This is a comparatively opulent expression of familial heroism. The aristocracy of design becomes the design itself, and is absorbed into the mechanisms of consumption. Consumers are not the beneficiaries of this mythology, but victims reciprocally defined as "outside" the tribe until they are able to participate in its legacy by buying into the Starck range.

This is Starck at his most subtle, but least ambivalent. A number of interviews with the designer over the past five years have fallen victim to proclamations of his disdain for the label-conscious, materialistic 1980s. In its place, Starck has proposed a "new" emphasis on what he has termed "democratic high fashion"; that is, high-quality, tasteful industrial design available to everyone. Unfortunately, this proposition lacks originality in its basic premise, blatantly harking back to the design principles of the Bauhaus and beyond that to the Deutsche Werkbund.

I AM calm
I SEE the invisible
I AM curious
I USE sparingly
I AM wise

**PHILIPPE STARCK, *GOOD GOODS***

Within this context the 1998 *Good Goods* catalogue is a self-conscious, marketing gesture, but one in which Starck redefines the role of the turn-of-the-millennium designer as that of paternalist whose task is both to guard and enrich society with his store of home-grown truths and environmentally-friendly products.

**"I ... TRIED TO find, COLLECT, CORRECT, OR CREATE (WHEN NECESSARY) OBJECTS WHICH ARE HONEST, RESPONSIBLE AND RESPECTFUL TO PEOPLE. NOT NECESSARILY BEAUTIFUL OBJECTS, BUT good objects ...**

**AFTER RESEARCH AND SELECTION, VERY FEW PRODUCTS COULD MEET MY STRINGENT standards. YET, ALTHOUGH THE ONES I APPROVED WERE STILL FAR FROM MY IDEAL OF PERFECTION, THEY DID CONVEY A CERTAIN spirit: AN ALTERNATIVE DIRECTION, A NEW WAY OF BEING."**

PHILIPPE STARCK, *GOOD GOODS*

Not all the catalogue's products were designed by Starck himself, but all of the approximately 200 items are included under his immediate auspices. The catalogue opens with a selection of organic foods, including wine, basmati rice, spaghetti, biscuits and organic champagne produced by OAO. Then comes a selection of eco-clothing; wardrobe "prototypes" "already familiar to the collective memory" and available in basic colours only. All the garments boast a "No Creation, No Chemical" mark, woven of organically grown cotton and containing a politically correct, promotional tagging.

The "9 months T-Shirts" designed by Patricia Bailer are the cleverest and indeed the most saleable of this lot, while the rain gear, albeit functional, urban and "properly" synthetic, serves largely once again to ennoble the designer himself with titles such as: "Wet Angel Starck", "Wet Duke Starck" and "Wet Elegance Starck". In addition to shampoos, creams, fly swats, cutlery, appliances, linens and a new range of Starck paints, the catalogue offers little more than a selection of comparatively more-affordable Starck classics such as the Miss Sissi lamp manufactured by Flos (1991), an array of well- and slightly lesser-known Alessi products (e.g. Dr. Cheese toothbrush, 1998), the Ola telephone by Thomson (1996), and the ubiquitous Excalibur loo brush (1996, Heller). One of Starck's newest chairs, La Marie (1997, Kartell) is shown to its advantage within an assortment of easily manufactured and therefore affordable plastic household artefacts which also includes varieties of the Lord Yo (produced by Fedra, 1994) and Cheap Chic (XO, 1997) chairs, and the Prince Aha stool (Kartell, 1996). Two of the most politically compelling items available for sale through the catalogue are the Respirator with three separate filters (both normal- and large-capacity for chemical impurities, and one "dust and particle filter including radiological dust"), and the now infamous TeddyBearBand [sic] which sports a head-like, cuddly-toy mutation on all but one of its appendages.

Taken overall, the *Good Goods* catalogue is a mission statement; a political mandate encouraging fidelity, family values, home decoration and the pursuit of the clean life, in addition to an apocalyptic vision of self-protection against all invading impurities, including the socio-political, if not ethnic "other". As a transparent marketing strategy it is immensely politically correct. It is unequivocally directed towards the middle classes whose political and economic bearings are such that they will decode its hidden assumptions and comprehend its neo-conservative messaging. In *Good Goods*, Starck expresses a series of socio-economic stereotypes and propagates the notion that what is good for them is something he will supply or can be supplied under his tutelage. In the introduction to the catalogue he claims to interrogate the basic terms by which we culturally construct relationships between products and consumers, but because of the strategic bias of the catalogue his isn't an efficient argument.

Further, *Good Goods* is not at all the "revolutionary manifesto" Starck claims. It is an essay in design in the mass media, the more so when taken in conjunction with its marketing web site: "www.goodgoods.tm.fr". The site is a means of disseminating and popularizing Starck images and propaganda. Prescriptively, it purports cultural artefacts which can be quickly distributed, are cheap and cheerful, and which imbue their audience with a "moral" aesthetic. The site is a profitable form of mediation between a "mass audience" and Starck, but because communication remains one-directional its democratic value is necessarily limited. Its long-term users who buy and then replenish will continue to be "consumers of culture" and trend seekers. The experience of ownership is still qualitative, not quantitative; dispensed to a select few, rather than the collective of mass spectators. The audience will not be a "free and unincorporated tribe of non-consumers" as Starck hopes, but will be socially fragmented by their own purchasing power. Providing the opportunity to buy cannot guarantee increased sales, regardless of the purported ideological premise.

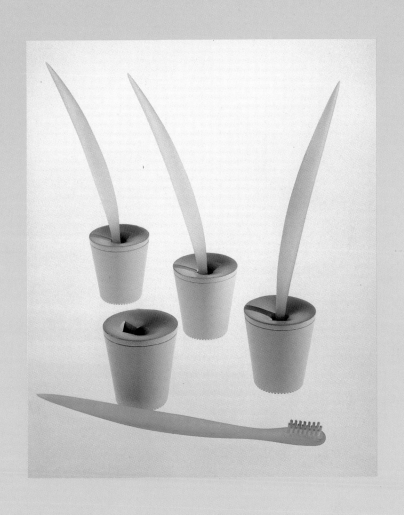

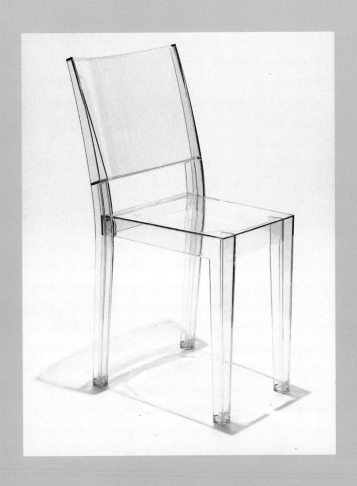

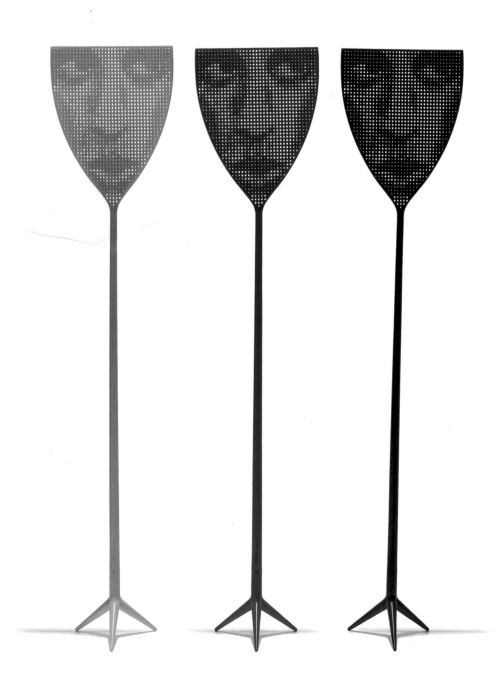

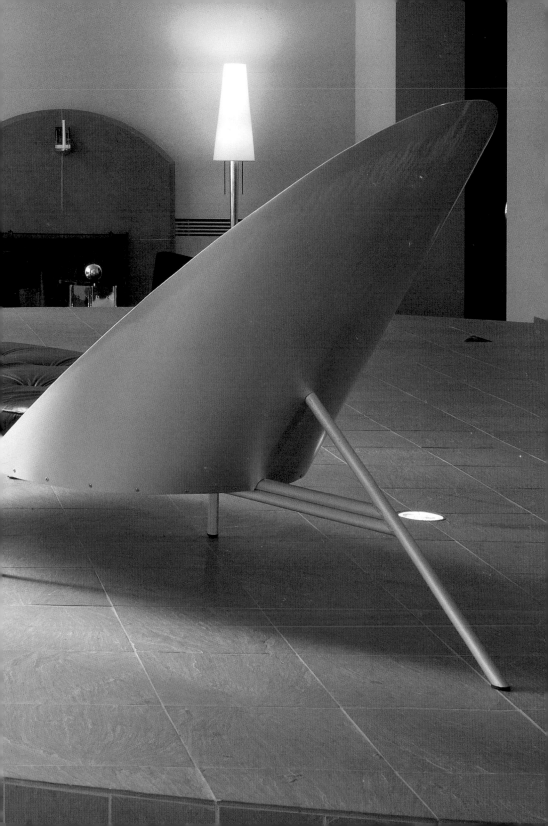

WITH
**LA REDOUTE**

---

**OAO: nous sommes ce que nous mangeons.** L'homme est un écosystème où l'esprit est indissociable du corps et de sa nourriture, dans une relation d'intime interdépendance. S'il est largement admis que l'alimentation a une influence sur la santé du corps, il est tout de même curieux que l'on ne reconnaisse pas aussi communément son rôle vis-à-vis de la qualité de la pensée. La gamme de produits OAO est un accès créatif à une nourriture organique moderne. Son intégrité biologique est garantie par le laboratoire Lima Expert, précurseur de l'alimentation organique, qui assure depuis plus de 40 ans une sélection rigoureuse de ses aliments biologiques. L'alimentation biologique sera – hélas – une mode, mais elle laissera un acquis important: une nouvelle norme de qualité alimentaire. Lorsque l'on peut manger de la nourriture ayant poussé dans un sol non traité aux engrais industriels et n'ayant subi aucun adjuvant chimique, il ne faut pas hésiter. Meilleurs pour la santé, les produits bio nous permettent aussi de retrouver des goûts que l'on avait tendance à oublier. OAO, mangeons intelligent. OAO. We are what we eat. Man is an ecosystem in which mental synergy is an integral part of the body and its food: a web of intimately interdependent and intertwined processes. Oddly enough, although it seems to be commonly accepted that diet has an influence on physical health, people are reluctant to acknowledge its impact upon mental energy. The OAO product line is a creative approach to modern organic self-care. Its biological integrity has been tested by Lima Expert laboratories, foundation-layers for organically produced foods. For over 40 years, Lima has been setting standards for organically grown naturally processed foods. Unfortunately the "health food craze" will turn out to be a mere passing fad. But it will have left an imprint on the way we evaluate what we eat. When it is possible to obtain products free of any chemical additives, which have been grown in soil uncontaminated by industrial fertilizers, we should not hesitate. You will find that organic foods are not only healthier: they are tastier as well. OAO, eat smart.

**A. Produit:** huile d'olive Sei Colli OAO, **partenaire:** Lima Expert, **description:** huile à base d'olives issues de l'agriculture biologique récoltées à la main, première pression à froid, **contenance:** 1 x 75cl, **référence:** 968.3577, **prix:** 99 F/14,93 Euros (prix au litre 132 F/l - 19,91 Euros/l).

**B. Produit:** huile d'olive San Vito OAO, **partenaire:** Lima Expert, **description:** huile à base d'olives issues de l'agriculture biologique récoltées à la main, première pression à froid, plus rare et délicate que la Sei Colli, **contenance:** 1 x 75cl, **référence:** 968.3585, **prix:** 119 F/17,94 Euros (prix au litre 159 F/l - 23,92 Euros/l).

**C. Produit:** riz thai mi-complet OAO, **partenaire:** Lima Expert, **description:** riz thai mi-complet issu de l'agriculture biologique, **poids:** 6 boîtes x 500g, **référence:** 956.3954, **prix:** 89 F/13,42 Euros (prix au kilo 29,67 F/kg - 4,47 Euros/kg).

ORGANIC
THAI RICE

**D. Produit:** riz basmati complet OAO, **partenaire:** Lima Expert, **description:** riz basmati complet issu de l'agriculture biologique, **poids:** 6 boîtes x 500g, **référence:** 956.3717, **prix:** 89 F/13,42 Euros (prix au kilo 29,67 F/kg - 4,47 Euros/kg).

ORGANIC
BASMATI RICE

**E. Produit:** spaghetti mi-complets OAO, **partenaire:** Lima Expert, **description:** spaghetti mi-complets issus de l'agriculture biologique, **poids:** 12 boîtes x 500g, **référence:** 956.4187, **prix:** 119 F/17,94 Euros (prix au kilo 19,83 F/kg - 2,99 Euros/kg).

ORGANIC SPAGHETTI

**F. Produit:** pâtes semini mi-complètes OAO, **partenaire:** Lima Expert, **description:** pâtes semini, à base de blé dur semi-complet issu de l'agriculture biologique, **poids:** 12 boîtes x 500g, **référence:** 956.7747, **prix:** 119 F/17,94 Euros (prix au kilo 19,83 F/kg - 2,99 Euros/kg).

ORGANIC
SEMINI

**G. Produit:** sel de sésame OAO, **partenaire:** Lima Expert, **description:** condiment à base de graines de sésame grillées issues de l'agriculture biologique et de sel marin, **poids:** 6 pots x 100g, **référence:** 956.6746, **prix:** 75 F/11,31 Euros (prix au kilo 125 F/kg - 18,85 Euros/kg).

ORGANIC
GOMASIO

**H. Produit:** sel marin OAO, **partenaire:** Lima Expert, **description:** sel marin récolté à Noirmoutier, **poids:** 6 x 200g, **référence:** 968.3529, **prix:** 49 F/8,90 Euros (prix au kilo 49,17 F/kg - 7,42 Euros/kg).

**I. Produit:** poivre noir en grains OAO, **description:** poivre noir de Madagascar issu de l'agriculture biologique, **poids:** 6 pots x 80g, **référence:** 969.3335, **prix:** 75 F/11,31 Euros (prix au kilo 156,25 F/kg - 23,56 Euros/kg).

ORGANIC
SEA SALT
ORGANIC
BLACK PEPPER

**B. Produit: Wet Prince Starck with K-Way, description:** redingote imperméable coupe-vent mixte, capuche intégrée dans le col, trois poches passepoilées, 6 boutons, fournitures métal hypoallergéniques, composition 60% polyamide, 40% polyester, **références:** ext. grège/int. jaune 809.3245, ext. anthracite/int. gris 809.3253, **tailles:** 1 (S), 2 (M), 4 (XL), 5 (XXL), **prix:** 890 F/134,30 Euros.

**C. Produit: Wet Duke Starck with K-Way, description:** veste longue imperméable coupe-vent mixte, capuche intégrée dans le col, trois poches passepoilées dont une poitrine, 5 boutons, fournitures métal hypoallergéniques, composition 60% polyamide, 40% polyester, **références:** ext. gris/int. jaune 809.1587, ext. anthracite/int. gris 809.3059, **tailles:** 1 (S), 2 (M), 4 (XL), 5 (XXL), **prix:** 850 F/128,17 Euros.

18

19

**Wet Elegance Starck with K-Way.** La ligne Wet Elegance est conçue pour vous rendre un pur service, mais de façon différente. Il m'a semblé en effet remarquer une malédiction du vêtement "de sport", ayant la triste destinée de péluter les paysages avec des couleurs criminelles, le "fun" ne m'a jamais fait rire. Il m'a semblé aussi possible que nécessaire de proposer des vêtements parfaitement fonctionnels, mais dans un autre registre, se référant plutôt à une élégance urbaine et moderne. Wet Elegance est une ligne au dessin classique, "retloué", d'un prix abordable, ayant les mêmes compétences pratiques que les équivalents: légèreté, imperméabilité, coupe-vent. Une matière de synthèse est, pour le moment, seule en mesure de satisfaire à ces critères. Avec K-Way, marque emblématique, inventeur du coupe-vent, nous avons développé un tissu à reflets changeants, à la fois imperméable, respirant, et facile d'entretien. Nous ne sommes pas condamnés à la vulgarité.

**Starck with K-Way Wet Elegance.** The Wet Elegance line was embarked upon to right a long-neglected wrong. I must not be the only one to have noticed that casual clothing is beset by a curse, compelling it to pollute the scenery with offensive colors. Garish hues have never amused me. I also felt it was both possible and necessary to make available completely functional clothing which takes its cue from an urban, modern concept of elegance. Wet Elegance is characterized by purity and classicism at an affordable price range and with the same practical virtues as its peers: lightweight, waterproof, a windbreaker. Synthetic fibres are the only choice which fulfill these criteria at the moment. Working with K-Way, whose name is synonymous with windbreakers in France, we have developed a waterproof, air permeable fabric with a wet look finish, easy to maintain. We are not doomed to vulgarity.

**Design.** Philippe Starck, **produits:** ligne Wet Elegance Starck with K-Way, **fabricant:** K-Way, **date de conception:** 1997, **date de production:** 1998.

**A. Produit: Wet Lord Starck with K-Way, description:** veste imperméable coupe-vent mixte, trois boutons, capuche, fournitures métal hypoallergéniques, composition 60% polyamide, 40% polyester, **références:** ext. gris/int. jaune 808.3096, ext. anthracite/int gris 808.3827, **tailles:** 1 (S), 2 (M), 4 (XL), 5 (XXL), **prix:** 790 F/119,12 Euros.

**D. Produit: Wet Angel Starck with K-Way, description:** long imperméable coupe-vent mixte, col officier indoublé, deux poches couture côtés, fente côtés, plis plat ouverts, fermeture par zip, sans capuche, fournitures métal hypoallergéniques, composition 60% polyamide, 40% polyester, **références:** ext. grège/int. jaune 808.7887, anthracite/int gris 808.8322, **tailles:** 1 (S), 2 (M), 4 (XL), 5 (XXL), **prix:** 790 F/ 119,12 Euros.

**E. Produit: Wet Ghost Starck with K-Way, description:** long imperméable coupe-vent mixte, capuche, fermeture par zip et rabat 2 boutons-pression, deux poches couture côtés, coin intérieur gauche rabattable (bouton-pression), fournitures métal hypoallergéniques, composition 60% polyamide, 40% polyester, **références:** ext. grège/int. jaune 809.0246, ext. gris/int. jaune 809.0351, **tailles:** 1 (S), 2 (M), 4 (XL), 5 (XXL), **prix:** 975 F/147,07 Euros.

Tous les Starck with K-Way en 24h chez vous: +80 F / 12,06 Euros.

---

26

27

**A. Crème hydratante Starck with Bioderma™, description:** flacon-pompe 250 ml. **référence:** 811.3998, **prix:** 125 F/18,83 Euros (34 F/dl – 7,14 Euros/dl)

**B. Eau nettoyante Starck with Bioderma™, description:** flacon-pompe 250 ml. **référence:** 675.9220, **prix:** 85 F/12,82 Euros (34 F/dl – 5,13 Euros/dl)

**E. Gel nettoyant moussant Starck with Bioderma™, description:** flacon-pompe 250 ml, **référence:** 689.1934, **prix:** 85 F/12,82 Euros (34 F/dl – 5,13 Euros/dl)

Tous les Starck with Bioderma en 24h chez vous: +80 F/ 12,06 Euros.

**C. Crème jour les mains Starck with Bioderma™, description:** flacon-pompe 250 ml.

**D. Shampooing doux quotidien Starck with Bioderma™, description:** flacon-pompe 250 ml.

**Starck with Bioderma™.** La gamme Starck with Bioderma™ est le résultat de ma rencontre avec Annie Vinche, à la tête du laboratoire Bioderma™.

### "BU BU"

"Bu Bu" stool, 1991, plastic, manufactured by XO.

### OYSTER BAR

Peninsula Hotel, Kowloon, Hong Kong, 1994.

### "W.W. STOOL"

Aluminium stool designed for the German film director Wim Wenders, produced by Vitra from 1990.

### ROYALTON HOTEL

Interior, New York, 1988.

### "HOT BERTAA"

"Hot Bertaa" kettle, 1990–91, plastic and aluminium, manufactured by Alessi.

### FELIX BAR

Peninsula Hotel, Kowloon, Hong Kong, 1994.

## PHILIPPE STARCK

The designer hung on the "Hooktoo" among his "Faitoo" range of kitchenware, 1996, for Alessi.

## PERSONAL HYGIENE PRODUCTS

LEFT: from left, Dr Spoon ear spatula; Dr Kiss toothbrush; Dr Kleen toothpick; Dr Cheese interdental brush, all 1998.
RIGHT: Dr Kiss toothbrush. All Alessi.

## "EXCALIBUR"

"Excalibur" toilet brush, 1996, polypropylene and nylon, manufactured by Heller.

## "COSTES"/"DR SONDERBAR"

LEFT: "Costes" armchair, 1984, steel tubing and bent plywood with mahogany veneer, manufactured by Driade.
RIGHT: "Dr Sonderbar", 1983, nickel-plated metal, manufactured by XO.

## "MISS DORN"/"DR NO"

LEFT: "Miss Dorn", 1985, tubing and black fabric, manufactured by Disform.
RIGHT: "Dr No" stackable chair, 1996, polypropylene and aluminium, manufactured by Kartell.

### "DR GLOB"/"SERAPIS"

LEFT: "Dr Glob" stackable chair, 1990, coated steel frame and polypropylene seat, manufactured by Kartell.
RIGHT: "Serapis" stool, 1986, steel tubing and mesh, manufactured by Driade.

### "CHEAP CHIC"/"LA MARIE"

LEFT: "Cheap Chic" stackable stool, 1997, aluminium and polypropylene, manufactured by XO.
RIGHT: "La Marie" transparent stackable chair, 1998, single-piece moulded polycarbonate, manufactured by Kartell.

### "PRINCE AHA"/"DR NA"

LEFT: "Prince Aha" stool, 1996, polypropylene, manufactured by Kartell.
RIGHT: "Dr Na" café table, 1997, SMC top with polypropylene and aluminium base, manufactured by Kartell.

### "DR SKUD"/"MISS SISSI"

LEFT: Dr Skud fly swatter, 198, thermo-plastic resin, manufactured by Alessi.
RIGHT: Miss Sissi table lamps, 1990–91, manufactured by Flos.

### "FAITOO"/"MANGETOO"

LEFT: "Faitoo" do-it-all range with "Hooktoo" rail, 1996, stainless steel, manufactured by Alessi.
RIGHT: "Mangetoo" cutlery and stand, 1996, stainless steel, manufactured by Alessi.

## "MISTER MEUMEU"/"JUICY SALIF"

LEFT: "Mister MeuMeu"cheese grater and spoon, 1992, stainless steel and polymide, manufactured by Alessi.
RIGHT: "Juicy Salif" lemon squeezer, 1990–91, aluminium, manufactured by Alessi.

## "TI TANG"/"JIM NATURE"

LEFT: "Ti Tang" teapot, 1992, white porcelain aluminium-coated, manufactured by Alessi.
RIGHT: "Jim Nature" portable television, 1994, high-density wood and plastic, manufactured by Saba.

## DELANO HOTEL

Interior, Miami, Florida, 1995.

## DELANO HOTEL

Miami, Florida. 1995. LEFT: Bedroom.
RIGHT: Interior.

## RESTAURANT FELIX

Peninsula Hotel, Kowloon, Hong Kong, 1994.

## RESTAURANT FELIX

Peninsula Hotel, Kowloon, Hong Kong, 1994.

## PENINSULA HOTEL

LEFT: Felix Bar, 1994.
RIGHT: Detail from bathroom, 1994.

## ROYALTON HOTEL

Lobby view.

## ROYALTON HOTEL

Interior views. LEFT: Bathroom.
RIGHT: Bedroom.

## ROYALTON HOTEL

Bedroom.

## ROYALTON HOTEL

Interior views.

## ROYALTON HOTEL

LEFT: Bedroom.
RIGHT: "Ara" lamps, in the lobby of the Royalton Hotel.

## PARAMOUNT HOTEL

New York, 1991. Bedroom.

## "GOOD GOODS" CATALOGUE

LEFT: Top, cover and, below, OAO organic products range.
RIGHT: Top, Starck/K-Way Wet Elegance water- and windproof
synthetic range; below, Starck/Bioderma Laboratories
skin and hair care product range.

## "STARCK NAKED"/"STARCK NAKED HOT"

1999, dresses, designed for Wolford, photographed by Jean
Baptiste Mondino.

# Picture credits

The publishers would like to thank the following sources for their kind
permission to reproduce the pictures in this book:

Alessi s.p.a 7, 25, 26, 27, 42, 45, 46

Arcaid/Richard Bryant 5, 58, 59, 60, 61, 62, 63, 64, 65, 66, 67/
   Earl Carter/Belle 48, 49, 50, 51/David Churchill 68, 69/Simon Kenny/
   Belle 2, 3, 8, 9, 52, 53, 54, 55, 56, 57

Carlton Books Ltd/Matthew Ward 1, 4, 30-40, 43, 44, 70

Flos Ltd 41

Jean Baptiste Mondino/Wolford 72

Purves & Purves 28, 29

Saba Personal Electronics 47

Every effort has been made to acknowledge correctly and contact the
source and/copyright holder of each picture, and Carlton Books Limited
apologises for any unintentional errors or omissions which will be
corrected in future editions of this book.

Thank you to Jo Leyland and the staff at Purves and Purves in London for
all their help with this book.